Glass House Visions

Skipping Stones and Baring Bones

Linda Ann Nickerson

Gait
House
Press

Published in the United States by Gait House Press.

Printed in the United States of America.

2023

Cover photo by Mor Shani on Unsplash.

ISBN: 978-1-7371383-4-1

GLASS HOUSE VISIONS

Dedication

Glass House Visions: Skipping Stones and Baring Bones is dedicated to the two most authentic people I have ever known.

Although they are as different from one another as any two people could possibly be in innumerable ways, they make a formidable team.

The stories inspiring a few of these poems are theirs, at least in part, but don't ask me which ones.

Pretense is not part of their vocabulary. Facades don't even enter the picture. They are who they are, and they're both pretty wonderful.

Strong, capable, brave, independent, bold, quality women. They're also hilarious, even if I don't get all their jokes.

I couldn't be prouder to call them my daughters.

GLASS HOUSE VISIONS

Initial Quotations

"Who that hath an hed of verre
Fro cast of stones war hym in the were."*
>> Geoffrey Chaucer, *Troilus and Criseyde*
>> (c1385)

"Whose house is of glass,
Must not throw stones at another."
>> George Herbert, *Jacula Prudentum*
>> (1651)

"Don't throw stones at your neighbors,
If your own windows are glass."
>> Benjamin Franklin, *Poor Richard's Almanack*
>> (1736)

* Translated, this means "He that has a glass head, beware of casting stones when he is at war."

GLASS HOUSE VISIONS

Preface

I live in a glass house. Maybe you do too.

OK, the house in which I live is not actually constructed of glass. But it might as well be.

What does it mean to live in a glass house?

It's impossible to hide in a glass house. Secrets are laid bare for all to see.

Metaphorically, this popular expression points to a vulnerability that is basically universal. We all live with some level of potential exposure. At least, we face the risk of that.

What if someone spots us in our PJs (or worse) or without our game faces on?

Are we the same people in private as we are in public?

Maybe we have some proverbial skeletons in our

closets. We know where the bodies are buried, though perhaps not literally. We might have secrets that scare even ourselves. Perhaps we have private stories, shadows, or sins – and we shudder to think that they might be discovered by others.

A glass house is never fully private, no matter how many shutters we shut. We can draw the curtains closed, but the shaky secrets still lurk within, waiting to be spotted.

It's easy to gather rocks to throw at others, whether in fun or fierceness. But it's dangerous. If we throw stones at others, we run the risk of return fire shattering our fragile glass windows or walls.

I live in a glass house.

My house (like most) has glass windows. It's easy to observe goings-on, especially when the blinds aren't fully closed at night. (We sometimes forget.)

We also have looking-glasses in a few spots. Maybe I need to preach more often to those mirrors.

But when I say my house is glass, it's more about

the fact that I have secrets and stories that can be scary to share. I know I'm not alone in this regard.

People are a curiously comical and quirky sort.

Observing ourselves and one another can lead us to intriguing insights and occasionally a bit of comedy (whether it's intentional or not). If we're paying attention, we might gain something along the way.

Let's have some fun, as we focus on all sorts of intriguing (and possibly partially fictional) folks. That's right. Not all of these memories are mine, nor are the bulk of the stories that are told in the pages that follow.

We might laugh and cry, grin and groan. We'll also uncover some memories (of both writer and reader), ponder deeper thoughts, and perhaps perform some self-examination.

Poetry can possess that power, if we give it the chance.

Welcome to my glass house.

GLASS HOUSE VISIONS

Glass House Visions

Skipping Stones and Baring Bones

GLASS HOUSE VISIONS

Table of Contents

Dedication iii

Initial Quotations v

Preface vii

Introduction..7

Abacus 15

Adding It Up..16

Allies for Life 17

Art Class Impasse 18

Bad Friends...21

Blowhard in the Yard..............................23

Boot Salute..24

Can the Plan..26

Character Captures................................27

Cheesy..29

Choice Matters.......................................30

Commercial Break 31

Compassion's Ration 32

Definitely Delayed..................................33

Exit Strategy 34

First Chair, Beware.................................36

Flying Figs 37

Fresh Face-off.......................................38

Fresh Start..40

Frittering and Jittering 41

From Zilch to Zing.................................42

Gift to Lift..43

Glass Houses...45

Gone for Good 47

Hide and Seek 49

Hurry Up, and Wait 53

Intruding on an Introvert.........................55

Job of Justice..57

Junk Jumbler (on Sweeping and Reaping) 58

Just Dessert 59

Kicking Appeals 61

Kick It Up 63

Kids Who Kid (The Bully Song)..............64

Knock-Knock, Who's Dare? 66

Ladies Can Lead 68

Let Sleeping Dogs Lie 69

Loaded for Beware 71

Loath to Linger 72

Look Out Below! 74

Missing Marbles 75

Mean Bean 76

Need We Say (Never) More? 78

Not-Me! 79

No Trace of Grace 81

Not Noticing 83

Overstayed on Cascade..........................85

Painful Process.......................................87

Pair-o-Dimes..88

Peace-Meal Nonet..................................90

Plunging with Aplomb..........................91

Pondering Placidity..............................93

Present..95

Quacking Up..97

Quads and Bods to Beat the Odds 98

Relay Repartee.....................................100

Reset in Motion....................................101

Revering Reveries................................103

Rot Off the Press.................................104

Run the Race..105

Rusted, Not Busted 107

Seeing Stars 109

Skipping Past Loom and Doom...........110

Surely Sung and Never Unrung...........112

Take That, Copycat.............................113

Taking the Helm 114

Tea It Up and Take a Shot 116

Testing and Protesting 118

Turbo Time 120

Undertow of Untruth...123

Upset Underneath 125

Value-Padded...126

Walk with Me 128

Well, Whee! 129

Whack-a-Mole 130

Wheeling and Reeling..132

Whirled Wide Web 134

Yea or Nay? 136

Yesterday's Yummies...138

Zealotic or Zesty 140

About the Author 143

GLASS HOUSE VISIONS

Introduction

Heads up for a whirlwind of variety.

As you read *Glass House Visions: Skipping Stones and Baring Bones*, you will find plentiful poetic forms and styles, such as:

- acrostic
- cascade
- haiku
- limerick
- monorhyme
- naisaiku
- nonet
- quatrain
- rondel
- saga
- sestet
- song
- tetractys
- and more.

You might even spot a ballad or an ode.

As a poet, I am often partial to the traditional structures of rhyme and meter. I love the challenge of working within these parameters. But you may find me venturing into uncharted free verse from time to time.

Analytical and literary-minded readers may seek to identify which poems fit each of these forms, while others may simply read on for pleasure and pondering.

These poems also run the gamut from satire to spirituality, from humor to heartache, from fact to fiction, from pointed to peaceful, and from deep meaning to deliberate mayhem.

Poetry lends itself to all sorts of approaches.

Some of these original poems have been previously published in print, online, or both. Many appear here for the first time.

Whose stories are these?

There's no easy answer.

Many of these verses have been drawn from my firsthand experiences or interactions with others. Others germinated from personal observations, daydreaming musings, or basic human nature. As with all creative writing (especially poetry and fiction), it's the wordsmith's prerogative not to reveal more specific details about original content origins.

Additionally, although many of these poems tell stories, others play with words and demonstrate assorted literary devices and techniques. More than a few combine all of these.

Who's speaking here?

Careful readers will find that the point-of-view varies from poem to poem.

Even those verses which are written in the first person are not necessarily autobiographical. And some pieces featuring the second-person or third-person point-of-view may be. That is to say that certain parts of these contents may be loosely based on personal experiences or relationships, but that is not always the case here.

That's part of the creative license that goes with crafting poetry or any form of creative writing. People are fascinating, and the most curious and quirky among us tend to appeal to writers' imaginations.

Occasionally, poems may appear to contradict one another. This may seem perplexing, until we consider how complex people can be. Even ourselves.

What about all those quotations?

I've include attributed quotations to accompany many of my own verses. Sources include well-known wordsmiths from classic literature and elsewhere. (Inclusion of cited statements within these pages does not necessarily imply endorsement of any of these speakers' full body of work.)

These quotes may be famous, familiar, or fresh to readers.

Employing literary license, I have occasionally

pulled these statements out of context, either for emphasis or irony. In lots of spots, these quotes serve as markers to remind us that even the simplest poems may be about more than they appear to be, if we look closely.

No finger-pointing.

Please don't attempt to recognize anyone you know in the lines of these poems. When subjects have been sparked by specific individuals or interactions, any and all identifying details have been altered or omitted.

In those verses that discuss or display life lessons or truths, readers are urged not to assume these are directly didactic.

Again, I live in a glass house.

And I'm often preaching to the mirror.

Please, don't anyone start picking up rocks.

GLASS HOUSE VISIONS

Glass House Visions

Skipping Stones and Baring Bones

GLASS HOUSE VISIONS

Abacus

Arithmetic advances beads.

Before your eyes, the answer reads.

Assign the numbers. Add. Subtract.

Count the cost, but don't react.

Understand the work at hand

Still surpasses what we've planned.

Adding It Up

I
Do
Not
Dare
Gauge
Anyone
Besides
Myself, if
Something
Critical is
Missing, so I'm
Taking a break,
Withholding my
Judgment. Still,
It is far too easy
To sum things all up,
Miscalculating and
Misinterpreting the
Missing pieces in some
Other man's life puzzles.

Allies for Life

Anybody

Longs for

Lenses

Into

Everybody's

Senses –

Finding

Or

Reminding:

Lifetimes

Insist that

Fondness

Exist.

Art Class Impasse

Invited to pull up a seat,
A studio session to meet,
The truth
    I'll confide:
I cringed,
    and I sighed
And hastened to beat my retreat.

The teacher arranged a sweet vase
With flowers assembled in place.
My cohorts
    drew fine,
While I
    sipped the wine
And stared at my easel's blank space.

My languid attempt drew a glare.
The master arose from his chair.
He paced,
    and he huffed.
He stomped,
    and he scuffed.
My still life drove him to despair.

I dabbled and dabbed with the paint.
(Remember, a Rembrandt I ain't.)
The blooms
    impish seemed,
The vase
    unredeemed.
My canvas begged high-pitched complaint.

The merciful end came at last.
I glanced at my painting, aghast.
The colors
    betrayed
Unspoken
    tirade.
I had to get out of there fast!

To draw, paint, or sculpt is a gift.
The artistic muse left me stiffed.
I don't mean
    to kvetch,
But attempting
    a sketch?
The mere thought can send me adrift.

Perhaps we may each have a flair,

With talent and passion to spare.
But I'll be
    the one
Who's coming
    undone
With art to complete and compare.

"When I discover who I am, I'll be free."
             Ralph Ellison, *Invisible Man*
                  (1952)

Bad Friends

The worst of friends will tell me
What I never wish to hear.
Thus doing, they dispel me
Of the things I once held dear.

They aren't afraid to pop me
When I'm all puffed up in pride.
They never fail to stop me
When I join the other side.

My bad friends never leave me
When my good ones come to play.
Instead, they call and grieve me
When I wish they'd go away.

Perhaps I have it backward;
I've considered it all wrong.
Despite the leading of the herd,
My bad friends make me strong.

They push me, and they prod me
With persistence and concern –
Encourage and applaud me

On occasions when I learn.

My vision's finally clearing,
As I thought it never would.
My bad friends are endearing;
Hey, my bad friends must be good!

"I don't need a friend who changes when I change
and who nods when I nod; my shadow does that
much better."

Plutarch
(1st Century AD)

Blowhard in the Yard

My neighbor's demeanor's like ice –
Gives answers unkind, imprecise.
He'll stop, stand, and stare
With nary a care,
And won't take his own bad advice.

When pigs fly, he'll take out his trash.
He may even burn up his stash.
The scents from his deck
Bounce like a bad check,
So daily our teeth we do gnash.

And still, as he passes, I wave,
But hope he'll go back in his cave.
He won't be ignored,
For he's on the board,
So all of us have to behave.

Boot Salute

Some swashbucklers suppose they're smart.
They act as friends,
    then break your heart.
Let language be most absolute –
No subtleties:
    give them the boot.

A friend more genuine,
    you know,
Will listen closely,
    toe to toe.
No languid promises unkept,
Nor boundaries yet overstepped.

May truth arise,
    that we discern
Which bonds to keep
    and which to burn.
Will be reboot and still remain
With those who will our friendship feign?

Kick up your heels.
    Do not delay.

Souls insincere may slip away.
For such, we need no ballyhoo.
Just whisper, as you leave them, "Shoo!"

"The world breaks everyone, and afterward, many
are strong at the broken places."
Ernest Hemingway, *A Farewell to Arms*
(1929)

Can the Plan

Oops.
Efforts,
Energy
May be wasted.
Purity of planning brings truth to light.

Can a hero make a clean getaway,
If his efforts
Leave white space
Where hope
Flees?

"It's the possibility of having a dream come true
that makes life interesting."

Paolo Coelho, *The Alchemist*

(1988)

Character Captures

Our neighbor needs to find her way
To avocation, pastime, play.
The handwriting is on the wall
Each day for her to scan, eyeball.
She sets her sights on our chalet.

Her name is Faith. Perhaps it fits,
Though her eavesdropping never quits.
She captures us within her glass.
Her snooping does the pale surpass.
We surely are beyond our wits.

Our routines, random though they be,
Display across the landscape free.
She takes them in, though it seems strange.
Her nosiness may never change.
On this the family does agree.

Our feathers fly at her charade.
She sees us glance and pulls the shade,
Perhaps to polish her device.
We might report, but we think twice
Before beginning a crusade.

Let's give her something, bait her hooks
With something worth her second looks.
Come, family, we have roles to play.
She cannot bear to glance away.
Let's stage a scene to break the books.

"The world is full of obvious things which nobody
by any chance ever observes."
Arthur Conan Doyle, *The Hound of the Baskervilles*
(1902)

Cheesy

Chewy, crunchy

Hunks of joy.

Every bite

Employ, enjoy.

Savor flavor:

You'll not cloy.

"Poets have been mysteriously silent on the subject of cheese."

GK Chesterton, *Alarms and Discursions*
(1910)

Choice Matters

You can offer someone sustenance,
Who may not eat or drink.
You can gift a person knowledge,
But you cannot make him think.

You can't make a person raise up,
If he'd rather choose to sink.
And a brand-new start means little
To the one who likes his stink.

"She had been too busy wishing things were
different to find much time to enjoy things as they
were."

Eleanor H. Porter, *Pollyanna*
(1913)

Commercial Break

Often, it pays to pay our respect.
Still, some days it's better to stop, disconnect.
A chair in the sun
Cannot be undone,
When needed perspective we must recollect.

Compassion's Ration

Compassion is a simple brew,
Poured freely – no return in view.
Yet some will try to top the tale,
Claim higher suffering, harsher gale.
They point to symptoms stronger still,
As if to best the one who's ill.
Such yammerers, they need not yelp.
Real patients seek much truer help.

Definitely Delayed

Apologies. I may be late.
My drive is dilatory. Great.
I will arrive
Past time. Take five.
I'm on my way, at any rate.

The beast that guards the clock is off.
Methinks he took a frothy quaff.
My timing quit.
I must admit.
And so I beg you not to scoff.

Priorities bid me to rush.
But calendars are prone to crush.
Excuses fail,
Beyond the pale.
The best that I can do is blush.

Exit Strategy

The blinker's on. Let's kick some dust.
We've gotta go. We simply must.
I cannot see. Could be the glare,
But I could swear that guy's a bear.
Our exit strategy's a bust.

Commuting doesn't top my list,
And here's another tricky twist.
That creepy guy there, all alone,
Just pointed at us with his phone.
Click his face too. I must insist.

Is he a felon, skilled in crime?
A crook who'd harm you for a dime?
Whatever ill he may have planned,
We've no desire to learn firsthand.
Speed on. We're running out of time.

This street may fright and flabbergast.
It's grisly here. We've been harassed.
Past memories fade;
New nightmares made.
Here comes our exit now. At last!

But wait. He follows us for more.
He's put his pedal to the floor.
He's trailing us on every turn,
And down our block, we're stem to stern.
Whoa. He's our neighbor, right next door.

But then, we have been wrong before.

First Chair, Beware

Perhaps the pretty teacher's pet,
Too petulant, yet never threat –
She led the class,
Jumped to surpass,
But was the first we might forget.

A century ago, she might
Have pleased instructors with delight,
Yet now it seems,
The crop's best creams
Are young smart alecks impolite.

Retort's the mode
And flip's supreme.
We've gone off-road
And doused the dream.

Can we return,
Perhaps unlearn –
And sweet or stern,
The tables turn?

Flying Figs

My friend's fictitious, absolute.
She's telling tales with bitter fruit.
I'm not sure why she singled me;
Perhaps we simply disagree.

Her lips, she puckers like a prune
To sing her altercating tune.
My closest chums dodge her debates;
Their daybooks fill with other dates.

We aim for higher raisin d'etre.
And so her stories we forget.
I know that I could flip my wig,
But I don't give a flying fig.

Fresh Face-off

My crew is real, authentic, sweet.
We take our masks off when we meet.
Though others think us rather odd,
We make no room for false façade.
Our trust o'er time has grown complete.

And though at times we disagree
With views that vary by degree,
We hug it out with bond secure,
And we our friendships reassure.
Respect is actuality.

The stories shared could curl one's hair,
As of our lives we freely share.
No gossip, dirt, or tawdry tales,
We weigh our words on wisdom's scales
To hold each other up in prayer.

So frequently we do perceive
Almighty does our cries receive.
His answers often beat our clock
And knock our feet from every sock
With blessings past what we'd believe.

We wish all friendships could be so,
But other ties do ebb and flow.
Relationships may disappoint
And send some noses out of joint.
True harmony most oft forgo.

"A friend loveth at all times, and a brother is born
for adversity."

(Proverbs 17:17, King James Bible)

Fresh Start

Filthy, foul,

Richly wrecked –

Every scowl

Scored and checked.

How can we come clean?

Stop and seek

Time-worn truth.

Awe's mystique –

Reclaims youth.

Trust the One unseen.

Frittering and Jittering

Tied to a chair with plates to spin –
He thinks his list may do him in.
His muscles twitch, a-chug-chug-chug.
He needs to move, to cut a rug.

The weather's whirling, wild and weird.
Alas, his gumption's disappeared.
His best resolve to exercise
Has vanished right before his eyes.

His own inertia bids him stay,
To hum and drum the day away.
Why does a list of chores to check
Stop him to stare, ask "What the heck?"

From Zilch to Zing

The stairway from boring to blight
Brings frustrated frowns back to light.
From grainy and chipped
To zany and zipped,
We zoom to the zest and ignite.

As zombies kept captive beneath,
No image of worth to bequeath,
We huddled and shook
As long as it took
Till false proved the evil one's teeth.

Our colors now glow without lamp.
Our spirits are no longer damp,
As boldly we stride,
No joys still denied,
For we from the gloom did break camp.

Gift to Lift

A hanky seems like scant relief
When offered in the thickest grief,
From woeful to worst,
Drift downward in thirst,
It yet may top one's very sleeve.

Still, somehow,
　　　as a hand reaches out,
Connection may
　　　righten our route.
The simplest small gift
A spirit may lift,
Relating a reasonable doubt.

Though rivers of tears may explode,
As we lumber under the load,
A mere word of peace
Can offer release,
And send us renewed on the road.

"We need never be ashamed of our tears."
Charles Dickens, *Great Expectations*
(1890)

Glass Houses

Glass houses
    bring secrets to light.
Fragilities flutter in sight.
No shutter or shade
Prevents their parade.
We live on display day and night.

As such,
    we must laugh all alone,
Reflecting on humor to hone.
The mirror will preach,
Though held at arm's reach.
No reason to cast the first stone.

Some stories
    and verses may sting.
A few contemplation may bring.
But here at the source,
Convicted of course,
We hope from the past to take wing.

"You look ridiculous, if you dance. You look ridiculous, if you don't dance. So you might as well dance."

Gertrude Stein, *Three Lives*
(1909)

Gone for Good

I choose to be happy.
    I choose to be whole.
I give up the faraway place
    in my soul.
The impolite hurting,
    who've knotted each scroll,
And livid attackers,
    who claim to control.

Electric excitement
    zips through every vein.
I'm bursting out laughing,
    releasing the pain.
My soul bubbles over,
    like drunk with champagne.
But what if the spoilers
    remount their campaign?

They won't simply vanish.
    That much is for sure.
Alas, for I know I can't
    banish each boor.
Still, though they may linger

and stay immature,
Their onslaught reverts,
    for my faith is secure.

(Remind me the next time
    they toss their manure.)

"Life appears to me too short to be spent nursing
animosity or registering wrongs."

            Charlotte Bronte, *Jane Eyre*
            (1847)

Hide and Seek

I must admire your technique!
You hide or seek or take a peek,
And yet I hear the words you speak.

Ideals like destiny and fate
Have caused your heart to hesitate.
But wait!
    Perhaps it's not too late.

Alas, you've chosen to withdraw,
To set your face
    and lock your jaw,
Although soon comes
    the great spring thaw.

It's time to toss away that doubt,
To loose the binds tied roundabout.
A new day dawns,
    so come on out!

A shiny glimmer crystal ball
Sheds just a shimmer,
    then a fall,

Ensuring never,
    not at all.

You say you're idle,
    in a shell,
As if the world outside can't tell.
But it's a self-made prison cell.

The wolf, he howls outside your door.
He beckons you to blood and gore,
The ever-present carnivore.

The sharpest fangs that drip with dread
Of those who'd keep you underfed
Can never harm you,
    sleepyhead.

For forces strong are standing near.
These multitudes,
    you cannot hear.
True trust can banish all your fear.

The dragon hovers, like a snake.
He hopes your soul to overtake.
And yet, you pray
    for Heaven's sake.

Somehow, you sense the answer deep,
As predators behind you creep.
Perhaps you sense it, as you weep.

For you are worthy of so much,
Although you crave the Master's touch.
Ah, faith is never just a crutch.

There's no deposit,
    no return,
For folks like us have yet to learn
That grace and love we cannot earn.

An open heart can grab the Gift
That mends and fixes every rift
With everlasting mercy's lift.

Again, I treasure your technique,
Although it be a bit oblique.
I wonder what it is you seek.

"Be courteous to all , but intimate with few. And let
those few be well tried before you give them your
confidence.
True friendship is a plant of slow growth, and must
undergo and withstand the shocks of adversity
before it is entitled to the appellation."

(George Washington,
"Letter to Nephew Bushrod Washington,"
January 15, 1783)

Hurry Up, and Wait

We're living in the Promised Land;
We're safe inside the gate.
Our life inside is simply grand;
It's "Hurry up, and wait!"

We race the pace to beat alarms,
To punch the clock in time.
With flapping arms and lucky charms,
We seek the finish line.

Delay the rooster's cry today.
We need to find some rest.
The years are spinning fast away;
This life is but a test.

So crawling from the covers sweet,
We sprint to face the day.
Until the calendar's complete,
We cannot walk away

Enduring just till Friday, then,
We muster what we must.
We're rolling much too quickly now

To gather any dust.

Delay the rooster's cry today.
We need to find some rest.
The years are spinning fast away;
This life is but a test.

This frantic pace grows young to old.
It makes us ever late.
And though we crave Olympic gold,
We hurry up and wait.

"All we have to decide is what to do with the time
that is given us."

JRR Tolkien
, *The Fellowship of the Ring*
(1954)

Intruding on an Introvert

"Ahoy! Who goes there?
        Reel us in,"
The eager skipper shouts again.
I bite the dust,
Although I must
Hospitably respond.
        Chagrin!

I shudder, as the boat he guides;
Too early were the changing tides.
Inside I know
I'd rather go
Where downsized company resides.

In bygone days,
        I craved the crowd.
I welcomed chatter,
        long and loud.
It seems of late
I hesitate;
I'd rather walk the row unplowed.

The landing party steps ashore.

My island's teeming with their corps.
Halt my routine;
I'll bear the scene,
Till they embark a-sea once more.

Job of Justice

Our joy to a job we may thrust;
To make many monies we must.
Yet finances fade,
And attitudes jade
When lonely for lucre we lust.

Employment may echo disgust,
And bounty may beckon to bust,
Unless we upgrade
With honor displayed,
Investing in much higher trust.

"A man, after he has brushed off the dust and chips
of his life, will have left only the hard, clean
questions: Was it good or was it evil? Have I done
well – or ill?"

John Steinbeck, *East of Eden*
(1952)

Junk Jumbler

With silent smirk and menaced mug,
She whisks the wrongs under the rug.
The carpet buckles from the load
Of dark details and debts still owed.

And those who tread upon that spot
May stumble, tumble,
    all for naught –
Though hidden ills, distortions deep
May disappear with one clean sweep.

Just Dessert

As children of all ages,
We eat our meals in stages –
All our senses on alert,
Looking for our just dessert.

Eating green peas, carrots, corn,
Waiting with a look forlorn,
Seeking something sweet to follow,
As reluctantly, we swallow.

If I eat what's on my plate,
Will you bring me
    something great?
Keep your beans and cauliflower;
Give me chocolate to devour!

Sweet confections,
    I desire.
My blood sugar
    may creep higher.
Still, I crave a sticky fix,
Though nutrition contradicts.

The best in life is worth the wait,
Although I just may hesitate.
I'll eat the vegetables accursed,
Or better yet, bring dessert first.

"Two worst things as can happen to a child is never
to have his own way – or always to have it.
Frances Hodgson Burnett, *The Secret Garden*
(1911)

Kicking Appeals

It takes some skill to toss a blade.
Add one or two,
    and be afraid.
These antics entertain the kids,
But sanity such tricks forbids.

The nimblest so may deftly dance
And leave the dangers all to chance,
While melancholy ones yet quake
And linger 'neath the veil opaque.

Bystanders wonder,
    watch, recoil.
I wait here for my blood to boil.
You crack your knuckles,
    chuckle, hoot.
Your trickery is absolute.

Oh, giggle, as you ply your skill
To carve the crowd
    to suit your will.
May sense prevail and notify:
Your timing may have gone awry.

So just for kicks,
    let's talk some smack.
Keep knives aloft,
    not in my back.

"A good laugh is a mighty good thing, and rather
too scarce a good thing; the more's the pity."
                Herman Melville, *Moby Dick*
                      (1851)

Kick It Up

Sometimes you gotta let 'er rip,
Get up and dance,
    cartwheel or flip.
This life's too short to sit and stew,
To nurse our woes
    or babbles brew.

Though rabble rousers irk and rile,
Just kill 'em with a certain smile.
Preserving joy
    and stepping light
Earns vic'tries larger than a fight.

Our dancing feet we much prefer
To gnashing teeth and flying fur.

Kids Who Kid (The Bully Song)

Before a child knows A-B-Cs,
He certainly has learned to tease.
He'll jab and jeer and joke and jest;
He has to prove that he's the best.

> We mock your face.
> We slam your clothes.
> We taunt your talk.
> We nag your nose.
> If you should balk
> At our low blows,
> We're only kidding.
> Don't you know?

For ever since the child was born,
Adults have treated him with scorn –
Each diff'rence loudly pointed out
Until they filled his heart with doubt.

> We mock your face.
> We slam your clothes.
> We taunt your talk.
> We nag your nose.

If you should balk
At our low blows,
We're only kidding.
Don't you know?

With acid word and sarcasm,
He ridicules enthusiasm,
Emulating those he knows
And maiming friends with verbal blows.

"But these things don't matter at all, because once
you are real, you can't be ugly, except to people who
don't understand.
                    Margery Williams, *The Velveteen Rabbit*
                                                    (1922)

Knock-Knock, Who's Dare?

Aye, dreams, they are fantastical.
Nigh days, though, chaos bring.
By mayhem's mix bombastical,
Why do mistakes upswing?

Chill. Marvelous and crazy treats
Fill up the books today.
Will favorite coffee, chocolate sweet
Still summon you to play?

In light, extraordinary sights
Spin wonders, call you out.
Then leave your blanket for delights.
Chin up, and walk about.

Come. Strange adventures beckon us
From hither off to yon.
Dumbfoundedness can be a plus.
Thumbs up, and let's begone!

"Yes, I am a dreamer. For a dreamer is one who can only find his way by moonlight, and his punishment is that he sees the dawn before the rest of the world."

Oscar Wilde, *The Critic As Artist*

(1891)

Ladies Can Lead

Fret not, though a female may stand at the helm.
Her goal is to pilot, not just overwhelm.
She captains the ship with a confident hand
Through waters unknown, though some
misunderstand.

Her visage is soft, but her countenance firm,
Committed to carry the journey long-term.
But the helmswoman wonders, along with her crew,
When may she receive equal pay overdue?

Let Sleeping Dogs Lie

Is it worth a try?
No shoulder to cry on here.
Better hold my peace.
Let sleeping dogs lie.
Better hold my peace.
No shoulder to cry on here.
Is it worth a try?

'Cross the bridge of trust,
We have shared our secret dreams –
Covenanted hearts.
Let sleeping dogs lie.
Covenanted hearts.
We have shared our secret dreams,
'Cross the bridge of trust.

I thought we were friends,
Every confidence locked safe.
I have been betrayed.
Let sleeping dogs lie.
I have been betrayed.
Every confidence locked safe,
I thought we were friends.

Never burned again.
Each entreaty I'll ignore.
Look the other way.
Let sleeping dogs lie.
Look the other way.
Each entreaty I'll ignore.
Never burned again.

"But I, being poor, have only my dreams; / I have spread my dreams under your feet. / Tread softly because you tread on my dreams."
 William Butler Yeats, *Aedh Wishes for the Cloths of*
Heaven
(1899)

Loaded for Beware

This pistol of a friend I've found
Wil step out with the gun's resound.
The pack behind, off like a shot,
She pulls the trigger, all she's got.

She makes her peace, right from the gate,
To run near four in thirty-eight.
And with both barrels firing fine,
She zips right past the finish line.

Though she's not packing on the street,
It's fair to say she brings the heat.

Loath to Linger

No leisure lady, I'd be lost
To sit a spell with both hands crossed.
I'd stretch and then in one fell swoop,
Leap to my feet to close the loop.

Yea, half-done projects leave me sore
And empty promises, much more.
Sure, rest and ease enhance one's state,
But what if duties fall too late?

Distraction may sound like a fault,
Attention lost by life's assault.
Yet I contend a wand'ring mind
May lead to gems no others find.

So I will take my hurried pace,
The fits and starts, the winding race.
A busy life, with every turn,
Is no onlooker's own concern.

"Don't get up. Just sit a while and think. Never be afraid to sit a while and think."

Lorraine Hansberry, *A Raisin in the Sun*
(1959)

Look Out Below!

A fellow who often spoke ill
And fostered not greatest goodwill
Did step on his tongue,
While venting his lung,
And so took the nastiest spill.

Missing Marbles

We're missing our marbles
    and many dear things.
We can't find our glasses,
    our keys,
        or our rings.
We pick up our cells,
    give each other a call
To ask where our phones might have
    happened to fall.

Despite all these trinkets
    we seem to misplace,
Our friendship is something
    lost minds can't erase.
Sure, losing some stuff
    for a stretch is a pain,
But together we claim
    we still have half a brain.

Mean Bean

What's wrong with having more caffeine?
I read this in a magazine.
Oh, headaches, nerves, and lack of sleep:
One cup, and you can get in deep.

It's an addiction, like a drug.
I think I'll have another mug.
But make it black; I can't stand cream.
The holy bean, it reigns supreme.

It leads to ulcers in the gut.
I don't believe that scuttlebutt.
My acid reflux, that's from work
Because my boss is such a jerk.

Who cares, if I have coffee stains
Upon my teeth; no one complains.
We raise our cups each coffee break
With steaming lattes, wide awake.

I heard it causes dehydration.
So that's the problem with our nation.
Someone better call the cops;

We're loitering in coffee shops.

I drink with friends; I drink alone,
But never drink from Styrofoam.
The smoke is rising from my cup.
I simply cannot give it up.

So what's the harm in a little caffeine?
So what, if it makes me lean and mean?
I ask my family, what'll it be?
Will you have coffee, tea, or me?

Need We Say (Never) More?

It isn't our nature
    to notice a need.
Like newbies to kindliness,
    we often misread
The words yet unspoken
    and troubles untold.
We seal up our suitcases,
    go for the gold.

Still, nobody nurses
    malevolent grudge,
Like one shoved aside
    with a negligent nudge.
Our catchword is kindness.
    We aim to be nice
And never run out
    of extensive advice.

Perhaps with the mirror we should have conferred.
When somebody needs us, let's toss not the bird.

Not-Me!

I have a pal who's just pretend.
He's my imaginary friend.
Whenever I get in a fix,
I blame it on his bag of tricks.

His name's "Not-Me," and he is fun.
He plays his pranks on everyone.
And when my goose is nearly done,
Not-Me is up and on the run.

Who left the dog out in the rain?
Who put the gerbil in the drain?
Who scribbled on the windowpane?
It was my friend, Not-Me!

Who failed to empty out the sing?
Who stained the carpet with blue ink?
Who dyed Dad's sneaker socks bright pink?
It was my friend, Not-Me!

Who left the phone off of its hook?
Who tipped the dryer, till it shook?
Who tore the pages from the book?

It was my friend, Not-Me!

Who told our secrets to the town?
Who rumpled up Mom's favorite gown?
Who tracked the floor in steps of brown?
It was my friend, Not-Me!

You see, my friend's a handy chap.
He saves me from the swat or slap.
If I just use my thinking cap,
I'm sure Not-Me can beat the rap.

No Trace of Grace

Eagerly, we fill our planners,
Waving still our angry banners.
We forget
Etiquette.
What has happened to our manners?

At the table,
    in the store,
On the freeway
    – hear us roar.
Rushed? You bet.
Ruder yet.
Each of us becomes a boor.

Courtesy has disappeared.
Kindness flew,
    as many jeered.
Witty quips
And bolder blips
Flaunt what our forefathers feared.

Still, we scramble to impress
When we ought to bow, confess.

Class-less clowns,
Earning frowns,
For our manners are a mess.

"Intelligence and courtesy not always are
combined; / Often in a wooden house a golden
room we find."
Henry Wadsworth Longfellow, *Poems*
(1848)

Not Noticing

I wonder, with all due respect,
How oft we overlook, neglect.
When troubles trounce a dear one's lot,
We shuffle by
    without a thought.

Why would we play a few cards shy
While offering just "Hi" or "Bye"?
We worry: Do we care enough?
Perhaps it's time
    to call our bluff.

Intent to help, extend a hand,
We simply do not understand.
Have we forgot just how it felt
To play the cards
    that we've been dealt?

"Be well," we toss a cheery word,
Not knowing that it sounds absurd.
Despite intentions best begun,
We grab our schedules,
    turn and run.

And in the mirror, I'm amazed.
I know the ante must be raised.
God help me, when one's chips are down,
To have a heart
    and stick around.

"It's much better to do good in a way that no one
knows anything about it."

Leo Tolstoy, *Anna Karenina*

(1877)

Overstayed on Cascade

"I thought we were roommates," they said.
But we're not.
A covenant of convenience is quickly crashed,
Like a motor piloted by multiple drivers … or none.

No radiant rhythm a helix undoes.
And winding ways
    whirl wanderers awry,
Leaving only rubber tread marks.
"I thought we were roommates," they said.

A borrowed corkscrew marks the place,
Recalling revelries
    and wild adventures
And pointing to fervent friends,
But we're not.

Coiling spirals may sound redundant,
Especially if uttered
    in a taxing rasp.
But the emphasis bears merit.
A covenant of convenience is quickly crashed.

When we skip our standards
    and merely improvise,
Where do we land?
If we ignore our allegiance,
    do we not become
Like a motor piloted by multiple drivers … or none.

Painful Process

Unscripted patience pains the mind.
The middle act is ill-defined.
Disquieted, we belt the blues,
Awaiting the director's cues.

And no one comprehends the text,
Reciting lines rehearsed, perplexed.
At last, we reach the final page,
When you-know-who
    steps on the stage.

She lets it rip and stuns the crowd,
Enunciations long and loud.
Despite confusion's giving pause,
The house, it rocks
    with mock applause.

Pair-o-Dimes

A penny might procure a thought,
If intellect could yet be bought.
And yet, to transform hearts and minds,
We need to change our paradigms.

In many quarters, most intense,
Majority may toss two cents –
Opinions subject to purloin,
Determined by a toss of coin.

Awareness now of simpler times,
When candy bars and tolls cost dimes,
Demands revisitation dear,
For that's a long way back from here.

Our currency has lost its gold.
Majorities are bought and sold.
We've turned the corner, past attack.
I think I want my nickel back.

"Not everything that is faced can be changed, but nothing can be changed until it is faced."
James Baldwin, *As Much Truth As One Can Bear*
(1962)

Peace-Meal Nonet

I'd like to order a fresh restart.
This menu comes up woeful short.
I've far too much on my plate,
So take a number, Ma'am.
No reservations.
The kitchen's closed.
Pull the blinds.
Ciao.

Plunging with Aplomb

I'll not be party
    to the throng,
To plant my toes
    in sod of wrong.
No chains contain
    the whimsy fair.
I'd rather soar
    and catch some air.

Enough reactions.
    No more gripes.
It's time to rest
    your rusty pipes.
I'll not bear
    pious bellyache
Or go paint on
    a grin that's fake.

It's time to take
    that leap of faith,
To spill the poison,
    plead the Eighth.
So, if you will,

give me a push,
And step back,
    as my swing sails.
    Whoosh!

Who knows? Perhaps
    I'll double back.
Momentum carries
    double clack.
But even so,
    I'll be unchained,
For by the best
    I have been trained.

"There is always something left to love."
    Gabriel Garcia Marques, *One Hundred Years of*
                 Solitude
               (1967)

Pondering Placidity

If peace is a river,
    then why are we tossed?
Like leaves in the current,
    we're whirled,
        double-crossed.
I crave to be colorless,
    vapid, and bland –
If just for a moment.
    you must understand.
Undoubtedly, soon,
    I would rise up and stretch.
I'd bring back my bouncy.
    My fervor I'd fetch.

We crowd,
    elbows jammed,
    as our times flow too fast.
Our joys are forgotten,
    our troubles broadcast.
Each shore that's adjoining
    the spot where I stand
May be solid ground,
    but it's not close at hand.

I wonder,
>
> how long till we come to a rest?

Perhaps it is time
>
> to put faith to the test.

Present

The victory and excellence
Belong most to the present tense.
A coin, flipped heads or tails, cannot
Move destiny to stronger spot.

The rules are pure and plain, my dear.
Though lawyers talk, they cannot hear.
In fact, the opposite occurs,
As fortune settles and defers.

Then, bored, the experts face the drive,
To push and pull,
    but ne'er arrive.
The habit echoes heretofore;
Pursuers profit nevermore.

The present is a joy, a gift,
And those who lose it pay short shrift.
Recalling and foretelling fail,
As life accelerates its tale.

"Ah! What is not a dream by day / To him whose eyes are cast / On things around him with a ray / Turned back upon the past?"

Edgar Allan Poe, *A Dream*

(1849)

Quacking Up

I think I may be quacking up.
It could be I'm just tired.
But looking at my face close-up
Leaves much to be desired.

The bags under my eyes are black;
This look I can't ignore.
I'm pretty sure that they could pack
A family of four.

The origami on my mug
No makeup may disguise.
But I accept it with a shrug,
As it full life implies.

"Time moves slowly, but passes quickly."
Alice Walker, *The Color Purple*
(1982)

Quads and Bods to Beat the Odds

We're growing quirky
    in our quest
To quell the quake
    and be our best.
No longer quick,
    our miles we run,
Though we admit,
    it's not much fun.

Our steps grow scarce
    in daily fog.
"Oh, my!" we cry.
    "We have to jog!"
Could quantity
    of exercise
Reduce the sags
    of guts and thighs?

We're fighting aging
    nail and tooth.
We won't let go
    of fleeting youth.
Becoming frail does

draw our rage;
We simply cannot
  act our age.

So Father Time
  we pacify.
We chuckle,
  as we wave goodbye
To naïve nods
  and childish dreams.
We wrinkle,
  but burst not our jeans.

"A bear, however hard he tries, / Grows tubby
without exercise."

AA Milne, *When We Were Very Young*
(1924)

Relay Repartee

No dialogue, just dueling jaws
With yammers,
    clamors, and guffaws –
A pair of clowns
Sparring for crowns,
They vie to win grandfather clause.

Unending tirades, on they drone
And interrupt
    to speak their own.
The world abides
And takes no sides;
We hold our peace with silent groan.

Why is it that these two antiques
With shrillest shrieks
    and flapping beaks
Persist unchecked
In disrespect,
As others guard their private piques?

Reset in Motion

My girls and I just broke some bread.
I'll share no secrets that were said,
Except to say
Without delay,
We're mostly glad the past is dead.

We choose the chance to chill and chug,
To raise a glass and lift a mug.
No time for fools,
Such friends are jewels.
We cry and crow and simply shrug.

To look at loves and labors lost,
To try each truth and count the cost –
We for a song
Do come along
To clear our chests at any cost.

Still, must we count the years a bust,
If by the trip we've learned to trust?
Each painful stroll
And shifty soul
Once thus examined, blows as dust.

In voices raspy, whispered woes
As errant chords do decompose.
Sweet music drifts.
Each spirit lifts.
And troubles fly where Heaven knows.

"There are some things you learn best in calm, and
some in storm."

Willa Cather, *The Song of the Lark*
(1915)

Revering Reveries

What dreams do we dare to forsake,
Refusing the risks we might take?

We soar while we snooze,
Then rouse just to lose.

Perhaps this is all a mistake.
I'd rather dream while I'm awake.

"Why, sometimes I've believed as many as six
impossible things before breakfast."
Lewis Carroll, *Through the Looking-Glass*
(1871)

Rot Off the Press

The news is extra, you can bet.
Its fiction casts a wider net.
Of facts, off-base,
No track or trace –
Let's give those folks a statuette.

Behind the scenes, they access gain.
They pick and peck past their domain.
Don't blink. Press print.
Oh, no. You didn't.
Our hearts are torn. They pour champagne.

As readers, viewers, they hoodwink,
They tap their keys; they nod and wink
To grab the scoop
And loop-de-loop.
The story's never what we think.

Run the Race

An epitaph is framed by years.
A dash appears between.
As loved ones gather,
    sharing tears,
One wonders,
    "What's it mean?"

A single stripe upon a rock
Denotes a lifelong path.
The dates do mark
    the lengthy walk;
Attendees do the math.

I want my dash
    to count for more
Than just an empty sign.
I'll run the race,
    from shore to shore,
Right to the finish line.

For life's a contest.
    Run with care,
A marathon to last.

And when we pass
    from here to there
We pray to be steadfast.

"Bid me run, and I will strive with things
impossible."

           William Shakespeare, *Julius Caesar*

           (1599)

Rusted, Not Busted

A vintage tractor long past prime,
I moved some mountains in my time.
Yet newer models have replaced
My usefulness, so I've been aced.

My stuff is lost; I cannot roar.
My turbo traction is no more.
They parked me here beside a weed,
Assuming I will go to seed.

But do I have to? Will I stall?
Need I a total overhaul?
Just mop the grime and grease away.
'Tis folly, but I want to play.

My total triumph would be toil,
A-digging through the deepest soil.
Invincible I claimed to be.
Why have they tossed away my key?

My temporary work rehearsed,
I stand beside the field, accursed.
My lamps reflect the sun, as prisms,

I'm seeking use, not skepticisms.

Tradition timed, vice versa calls,
Although my engine stops and stalls.
I want to work. I simply must.
'Tis better to burn out than rust.

"It's better to burn out than it is to rust."
Neil Young, "My, My, Hey, Hey (Out of the Blue)"
(1979)

Seeing Stars

I do not trace the zodiac.
I do not know my sign.
It's not that I want money back;
I wait for the divine.

As choices clamor for our eyes,
We focus where we may.
Our hearts do quickly improvise
To give ideas full sway.

The stars may tell a story, true,
For evil or for good.
And though I cannot speak for you,
They're oft misunderstood.

The future may surprise us all,
Assumptions tossed afield.
No matter what the cosmic scrawl,
The truth will be revealed.

Skipping Past Loom and Doom

Me melancholy? No, siree.
It's simply not my cup of tea.
I'm fine, you know.
Or does it show?
Perhaps it's merely repartee.

"Play nice," they say. I must object.
The rules were wrong, last time I checked.
Just to travail
And bring the mail
May stop the shuttle in effect.

From warp to weft, a lot is left,
When weaving through one's life.
The finest textiles fall to theft,
If subjected to strife.

I wanna fly with feathers high,
Escape to heal, re-fortify.
I'm living large
To stop, recharge,
And view a vantage by and by.

So labor's lost at any cost,
As workers may be too far bossed.
Unraveled threads
Bring hotter heads,
Thus, fortune's fools are double-crossed.

From warp to weft, a lot is left,
When weaving through one's life.
The finest textiles fall to theft,
If subjected to strife.

"The secret of happiness is not doing what one
likes, but in liking what one does."

JM Barrie, *Peter Pan*
(1911)

Surely Sung and Never Unrung

'Tis said you can't unring a bell.
Resounding gongs their stories tell.
The chime plays out. Sound the alarm.
Call constable, patrol, gendarme.

Appealing secrets bell the cat
And fill vain ears with dark chitchat.
They hollow ring, when once begun –
Take toller to the lowest rung.

So ring it up. Announce the charge.
For he who tolls is still at large.
Though he go jingling merrily,
Bell, book, and candle hold the key.

"It is only in vulnerability and risk – not safety and
security – that we overcome darkness."
Madeleine L'Engle, *A Wrinkle in Time*
(1962)

Take That, Copycat.

Can't stand it when she tells my jokes
To grab the spotlight,
    wow more folks.
She'll parrot lines
To show she shines
And earn their favor.
    Holy smokes.

Come up with your own tales,
    I muse.
Don't steal my stuff,
    so you can schmooze.
You may be loud,
But are you proud
To pirate humor to amuse?

Taking the Helm

Trials and tempests

All around,

Kinetic conquests

Inward bound,

Need no more protests

Gone aground.

Trim up the sails.

Hearken the whales.

Echo the tales.

Headwinds in flight

Earn our delight;

Lo, breakers bowl.

Merrily roll.

"I am not afraid of storms, for I am learning how to sail my ship."

Louisa May Alcott, *Little Women*

(1869)

Tea It Up and Take a Shot

Sometimes a chip lands in the drink
And sends us nearly past the brink.
We sip and spar,
And dream sub-par,
For nothing's ever as we think.

It's not that we'd improve a lie,
But some brews still
    a tongue may tie.
As roles reversed
Are unrehearsed,
We have to swing to qualify.

Forgive the metaphors I mix.
The game is rigged.
    There is no fix.
Simplicity's
My cup of tea.
And poets break the rules for kicks.

Alas, the tempest swirls the pot.
We're in the rough.
    Give all you've got.

Go get a grip.
And take a sip.
Another round
    brings food for thought.

"Hold fast to dreams, for without them, life is a
broken winged bird that cannot fly."
    Langston Hughes, *Montage of a Dream Deferred*
                             (1951)

Testing and Protesting

Most people are fearsome of failing,
Afraid of their weakness unveiling.
But a triumph is best
When it comes from a test,
And the struggler winds up prevailing.

For what treasure comes from a whim,
That gives up
    when prospects look dim?
Hang onto your hope
To walk the tightrope,
And crawl way out there
    on that limb.

Don't worry when folks are judgmental,
Or even if they're temperamental.
You follow the dance.
Leave nothing to chance.
Remember life's experimental.

So don't be alarmed by a trial
Or live out your days
    in denial.

Just jump in the game
For your highest aim,
And hold out for something worthwhile.

"There are better things ahead than any we leave behind."
CS Lewis, *The Collected Letters of CS Lewis, Vol. 3*
(1963)

Turbo Time

The beep explodes, amid our moans,
As overtired working drones.
We hit the snooze with groggy groans
And try to stir our weary bones.

We race the clock and blast therefore,
Departing madly through the door
To chase the daily tug- of-war,
So breakfast often we ignore.

The most important meal,
    some say,
Promoting health,
    not tooth decay.
And still we skip it,
    day by day,
To rev the car.
    Up and away!

A bagel toasted on the run,
A donut or a honeybun,
A sugared cereal to shun,
A non-nutritious day begun.

We grab a latte on the road
To percolate our overload.
With stomachs gearing to implode,
We dive into today's workload.

Of course, midmorning brings a spell.
And we begin to feel unwell.
A cup of coffee may propel,
As we await the noontime bell.

Perhaps we need an altered plan,
To catch up with the old Sandman.
We're overusing our time span,
But giving it the best we can.

If we could rise
    with time to spare,
We might have time
    to clear the air.
A quiet cup
    and breakfast square
Might help us daily
    to prepare.

For growling tummies just distract;

They cause our guts to overact.
They lead us off the path, sidetracked
And make us wish that we had snacked.

Tomorrow we'll get up in time.
We'll spring from bed at the first chime.
We'll dine on omelettes sublime
To gear up for the upward climb.

"After all, tomorrow is another day."
Margaret Mitchell, *Gone with the Wind*
(1936)

Undertow of Untruth

The waters whisper in your head
Of words convincing,
    full of dread.
The undertow may pull you down,
With words rolled by to make you drown.

Alas, a friend has proved untrue.
She's not unique in such purview.
The tide will drift.
    Send her adrift.
Waste no more moments being miffed.

A time-out cannot fit the bill.
So listen not to shell or shill.
No secrets sleep over your soul;
Her falsehood's out of your control.

Let us not undertake to boast,
No payback in the uttermost.
Such drama's not our downward spool,
For we completed middle school.

"An eye for an eye only leads to more blindness."
Margaret Atwood, *Cat's Eye*
(1988)

Upset Underneath

We measure not another's pace,
Pretending to a higher place.

For none can fathom what's below,
Barrage of blows or undertow.

The frailest, fearsome, feeble knight
May boldly battle out of sight.

His valor could out-measure ours,
As we salute our bars and stars.

It is only with the heart that one can see rightly;
what is essential is invisible to the eye."
                    Antoine de Saint Exupery, *The Little Prince*
                                            (1943)

Value-Padded

What respite does a victim need,
When he advice no more will heed?
He pads the bill
To have his fill,
Yet wonders why he can't succeed?

No getaway, no time to flee,
The sages say, "Just let him be,"
True values hold
Much more than gold,
And pearls purloined are mere debris.

Perchance it takes a pound of pluck
To rouse a rebel rogue who's stuck.
No shady deal
May horrors heal,
And easy money seals a schmuck.

"Pursue the things you love doing, and then do them so well that people can't take their eyes off you."

Maya Angelou, *I Know Why the Caged Bird Sings* (1969)

Walk with Me

Let's walk together;
Stroll by my side at midnight,
No one else around.

Whisper secrets here;
I will never tell a soul,
Except my own heart.

The moon lights our way,
Watching o'er the empty lane.
What could be better?

"Love makes your soul crawl out from its hiding
place."
    Zora Neale Hurston, *Their Eyes Were Watching
God*
(1937)

Well, Whee!

I've got a secret. I won't tell.
But it has made my spirit swell.
Don't ask. Don't peek.
Not gonna leak.
Just trust me.
    Things will turn out well.

I simply can't stay in my chair.
My mind, it zips from here to there,
Sit still? No way.
Not gonna say.
But soon wild wonders
    I'll declare.

"'And now,' cried Max, "'let the wild rumpus start!'"
Maurice Sendak *Where the Wild Things Are*
(1963)

Whack-a-Mole

I once was young, but now am old.
My skin hangs off my face in folds.
The old libido's growing cold,
And I see Doctor Whack-a-Mole.

This nasty physical assault
Is truthfully my own darn fault.
I should have known right when to halt.
Now I see Doctor Whack-a-Mole.

I loved the sun and summer fun.
I'd tan my skin till it was done.
But dots and spots their course have run.
So I see Doctor Whack-a-Mole.

A freeze-off here, a snip-off there,
Until my skin is clean and fair,
With tiny Band-Aids everywhere
From good old Doctor Whack-a-Mole.

Some biopsies may be required.
On such occasions, I've perspired
Until results have been inquired

Of dear old Doctor Whack-a-Mole.

And still I crave a sunny spot
To lounge and laze, do diddly-squat,
Although I'm sure, like it or not,
I'll soon see Doctor Whack-a-Mole.

If you are one who loves the sun,
Be careful. Here's the 4-1-1:
Rub on the sunscreen; use a ton,
Or you'll see Doctor Whack-a-Mole.

Wheeling and Reeling

Oh, uphill climb!
    I'm in a bind.
My energies are ill-defined.
Still, on I roll
To face each goal,
Though with each spin
    my gears go grind.

No melodrama do I bleat,
As kindly company I meet.
Lighthearted, they
May greet the day,
As I taste time's dust in the street.

With awkward effort in the sun,
Collecting muster,
    on I run.
Might you by chance
Have ant-filled pants,
Or do you go all-out for fun?

Opponents dear,
    I mean no harm.

Ride on, if I should sound alarm.
The clock ticks tock;
My frame does rock.
I fear that I might buy the farm.

The end is just around the bend,
Where volunteers refresh, attend.
Though I'm hard-pressed,
I dare not rest,
And soon this race I'll recommend.

"Beware, for I am fearless, and therefore powerful."
Mary Shelley, *Frankenstein*
(1818)

Whirled Wide Web

What fun we'd all
    go out and get
Before there was
    an internet.
No keys to tap,
    no mice to click –
No online games
    played super-quick.

No wild tantrums
    to unfold,
And those that did
    remained untold.
No need to mask
    our honest joy
At play, our senses
    to employ.

We'd hop on wheels
    and leap to tear
Against the wind
    to double-dare,
Swing willy-nilly

to the moon,
Or knot a wrist
　to some balloon.

Such tender times come
　with no plug,
Still we have shed them
　with a shrug.
We wonder why
　we're on the brink.
I guess we know.
　　Knock-knock. Wink-wink.
The world to screens
　did surely shrink.

Yea or Nay?

I used to link laws with beliefs
As metaphorical motifs.
Inside, I'd simmer,
    yelp, and yell
To ponder bliss and flee from hell.

I'd measure where I thought I stood
Between the camps of bad and good.
And maybe,
    if I did it right,
My steps would lead to endless light.

At last, I tumbled in the grass,
Regarded yonder,
    took a pass,
And yielded to the roar of grace.
'Twas anything but commonplace.

Considering my former stance,
I've stepped aside from duty's dance.
Though truth may grade not on the curve,
To rule on other's takes some nerve.

So thankful that I need not know
Who may belong above, below.
For that decision takes a crown.
My pay grade sits a long way down.

Yesterday's Yummies

I met a friend, long overdue,
To share a bite or three or two.
The conversation took a turn.
(You'd be surprised what you can learn.)

The fishing started with hors d'oeuvres
And quickly grated on my nerves.
She trawled, but I refused the bait.
I pushed the food 'round on my plate.

Undaunted and without regret,
Back-trolling, she did dump her net.
She popped and bobbed, as if for sport.
This chum of old, I failed to thwart.

The waitress brought the check at last.
I lured my angling friend out fast.
The lunch was tasty. We went Dutch.
The conversation? Not so much.

The moral of this story's end,
In case you have a selfsame friend:

When lured into lunch in a crunch,
It's better to follow your hunch.
Don't give in and toss out a punch,
Or she might get her shorts in a bunch.

Zealotic or Zesty

Zealotic as I used to live,
Though given often to misgive –
I'd hang with those
Who'd turn the nose,
But long would dawdle to forgive.

Bare truth can be a hazard deep,
As from compassion it can keep.
We may be right,
But wrongly bite,
If facts unchecked are all we keep.

I hope at last to hold my zeal,
And yet to sail more even keel.
A balance shift
Could be a gift,
If to the heart it does appeal.

"I have to remind myself to breathe – almost to remind my heart to beat."

Emily Bronte, *Wuthering Heights*

(1847)

GLASS HOUSE VISIONS

About the Author

An award-winning poet and prolific writer, holding a B.A. in English and an M.S. in Journalism, Linda Ann Nickerson has worked as a professional writer for more than four decades.

She has also taught creative writing, poetry, and literature classes and has presented to adult writing workshops and groups.

In an earlier life, she worked as a book editor and widely-read reviewer of books on all types of topics.

Linda Ann writes news and feature columns for several well-known websites. Her published portfolio includes well over 5,000 web articles, as well as countless print pieces.

When she's not writing poetry, fiction, news, features, or promotional copy, Linda Ann may be found riding horses, running canine cross-country, biking country trails, stitching up a quilt, or training for her next marathon. Or she may simply have her nose buried in another book.

Other poetry books by Linda Ann Nickerson include:

- *ABCs of Acrostic Poetry: The keyword is king*

- *Absent Nightmare Zinnias: Rhymed Acrostics from A to Z*

- *Fashion Victims: Missing Style by a Marvelous Mile*

- *Going Vertical: Acrostics in Action*

- *Horseplay Secrets: Learning in Rhyme from Equines Sublime*

- *Stealing Wonder: A Rhyming Race to Capture Grace*

- *What's in Santa's Sleigh This Christmas?*

GLASS HOUSE VISIONS

GLASS HOUSE VISIONS